It's the Little Things *for Mothers*

300 SIMPLE WAYS TO TAKE TIME OUT AND TREAT YOURSELF

KATE McBRIDE

Copyright ©2004, F&W Publications, Inc.
All rights reserved. This book, or parts thereof, may not be reproduced in
any form without permission from the publisher; exceptions are made
for brief excerpts used in published reviews.

Published by
Adams Media, an F+W Publications Company
57 Littlefield Street, Avon, MA 02322 U.S.A.
www.adamsmedia.com

ISBN: 1-58062-915-6

Printed in Canada.

J I H G F E D C B A

Library of Congress Cataloging-in-Publication Data
McBride, Kate.
It's the little things for mothers / Kate McBride.
p.   cm.
ISBN 1-58062-915-6
1. Mothers--Conduct of life. I. Title.
BJ1610.M4   2004
306.874'3--dc22   2003019613

Photographs courtesy of Image Source and Marlin Studios, 2002.

This book is available at quantity discounts for bulk purchases.
For information, call 1-800-872-5627.

This book is dedicated to Caitlin McBride,
my most beautiful and special daughter,
without whom I may never have learned
to appreciate the "little things" in life!

I would like to thank the following special women who generously contributed their ideas for this collection: Jule Rathjen, Julie Gutin, Tracy Quinn McLennan, Sandy Keefe, and Ellen Stobaugh.

An extra-special thanks goes to Danielle Chiotti, a most talented editor, who showed me that even 300 one-liners need a lot of editing and to Laura MacLaughlin, a most talented copy chief, who showed me that then they need a lot of copyediting!! Thank you both for your professional additions and creative touch.

"It's relentless, motherhood is. That's the most accurate way I can put it: relentless. Relentless in its demands, relentless in its joys. There is always one more car pool, one more tantrum over the wrong color sippy-cup, one more birthday party to get a bright-colored present for. Yet, God willing, there is always one more lopsided Popsicle stick jewelry box, one more smile from across the park, one more chorus of 'Mommy's home!'"

—Amy Krouse Rosenthal

Sing! Turn up the volume, dance, and sing your house clean—it makes the work fun and you just might burn a few calories, too.

Eliminate the phrase
"perfect mother"
from your vocabulary.

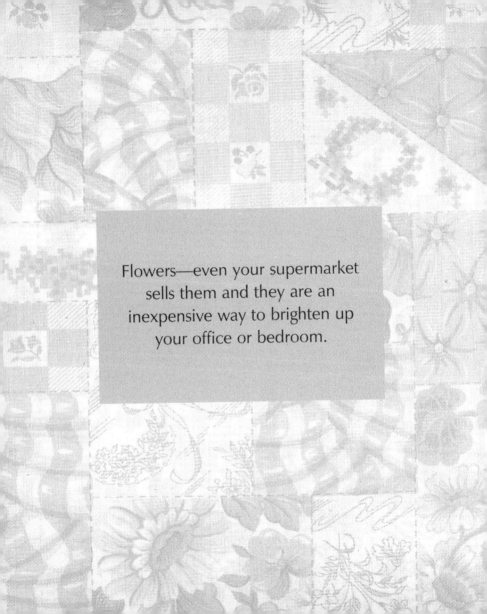

Flowers—even your supermarket sells them and they are an inexpensive way to brighten up your office or bedroom.

You won't get any training
for motherhood, so when you
make a mistake, forgive yourself
quickly and move on to the
next challenge.

Life gratitude list:

Make a list of all the things you are grateful for: your health, your child, special friends, your home, your job, etc. Use your journaling time to add to the list periodically—reflect on those things in your life that you feel lucky to have and add them. Keep it tacked to your refrigerator or tucked in your planner. A peek at this "gratitude list" can soften even the most stressful or frustrating times and put things in the proper perspective for you.

Gratitude list for the day:

We all have those days when there is one crisis after another and the whole day seems to be going down the tubes. Find a quiet place in the middle of the chaos and steal a moment to make a list for the here-and-now!

Write down at least five good things that have happened since you got out of bed this morning. This exercise will help you center yourself and you will be able to get through the rest of the day!

Be gentle with yourself.
Mothering is one of the
hardest jobs around.

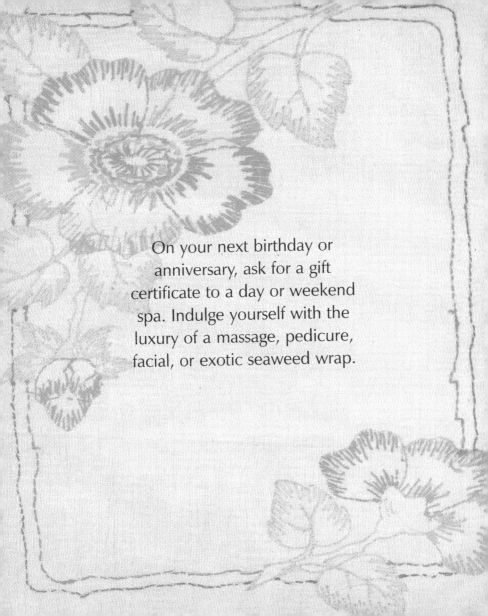

On your next birthday or anniversary, ask for a gift certificate to a day or weekend spa. Indulge yourself with the luxury of a massage, pedicure, facial, or exotic seaweed wrap.

The more organized you are, the more time you save—the more time you save, the less chaotic your day. Declare a day to clear clutter in your home and purchase wicker baskets or fun containers for simple, easy storage.

"If you have never been
hated by your child, you have
never been a parent."

—Bette Davis

If you are a stay-at-home mom, make sure you have at least one adult conversation every day. It's too easy to let days go by with no one to talk to but "the kids."

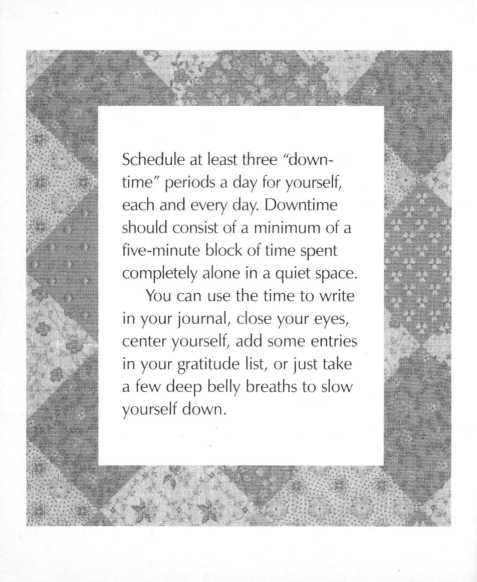

Schedule at least three "down-time" periods a day for yourself, each and every day. Downtime should consist of a minimum of a five-minute block of time spent completely alone in a quiet space.

You can use the time to write in your journal, close your eyes, center yourself, add some entries in your gratitude list, or just take a few deep belly breaths to slow yourself down.

Put yourself first—you will be no good to anybody else unless you are feeling your personal best.

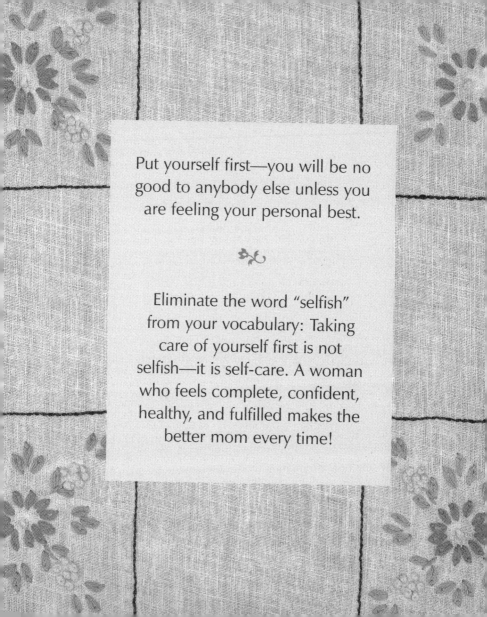

Eliminate the word "selfish" from your vocabulary: Taking care of yourself first is not selfish—it is self-care. A woman who feels complete, confident, healthy, and fulfilled makes the better mom every time!

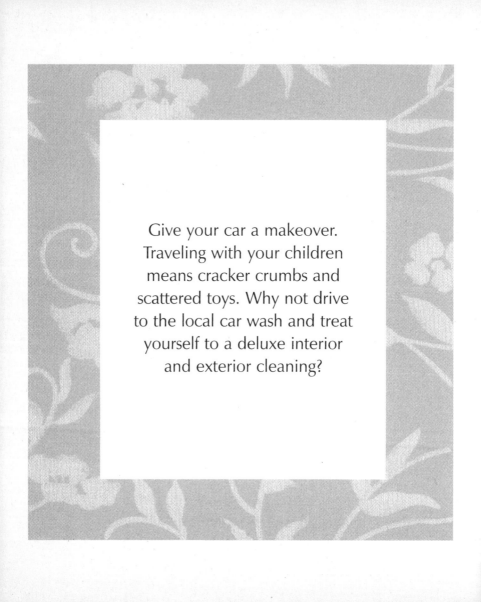

Give your car a makeover.
Traveling with your children
means cracker crumbs and
scattered toys. Why not drive
to the local car wash and treat
yourself to a deluxe interior
and exterior cleaning?

Stargaze. All you need is a clear summer night and a blanket. Feel the warm air on your skin and count shooting stars. Can you find Orion and the Big Dipper?

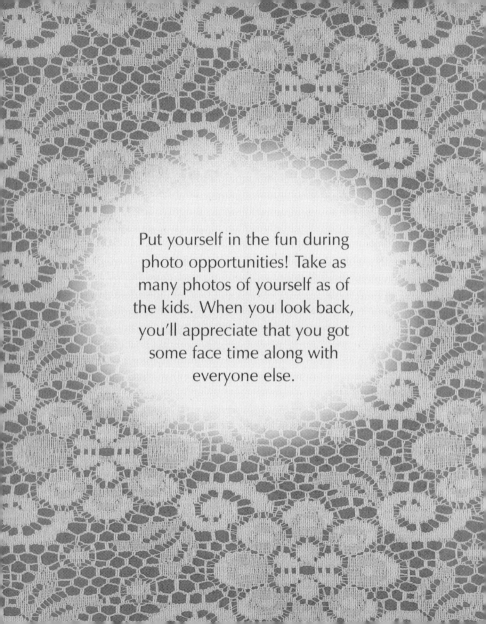

Put yourself in the fun during photo opportunities! Take as many photos of yourself as of the kids. When you look back, you'll appreciate that you got some face time along with everyone else.

Remember: the word "mom"
upside down is "wow."

Kitchen Shortcut

Inside-Out Ravioli

Here's a fast, easy, and healthful meal you can put together in no time that makes an impressive presentation after a busy day at the office. Bonus: The kids love it in spite of the spinach!

1. Cook and drain 1 pound of ziti or bow ties.
2. Cook 1 box of frozen chopped spinach; then drain well.
3. Sauté the spinach in 2 tablespoons of butter and lightly salt it.
4. In a big bowl, mix the drained pasta, the buttered spinach, 1 container of ricotta cheese, and a handful of grated cheese. Eat!

"I tend to allow my children
take risks to test themselves.
Better broken bones than
broken spirits."

—Rose Kennedy

The products made for babies are delightfully scented and gentle. Why not use them too? Wash your nightgowns and sheets in Dreft or use soft baby oil on your skin and baby powder in your shoes.

What should you do with that empty bedroom now that the kids are grown and have their own place? Take it over and make it over!

Create your personal space for a library, projects, fitness, or meditation, and have fun decorating it in your own style. Experiment with "extreme" design ideas that might be too daring for common living areas!

Take a picture of your child on her first birthday in a special place—under your favorite tree, on a bench by the lake near your home—that is meaningful to you. Every year on the child's birthday, take her picture in the same spot. Take one of the child alone and one with you.

This "pictorial history" is a terrific way to mark the changes in both of you and it is a keepsake your child will appreciate when she is grown.

*F*ill a beautiful wicker basket with watercolors, colored markers, a selection of lovely papers, and oil pastels. When you have a minute to yourself, curl up on the sofa and make whimsical pictures just for you!

Make original stationery for yourself—get creative with stickers, stamps, and pressed flowers. The sky is the limit!

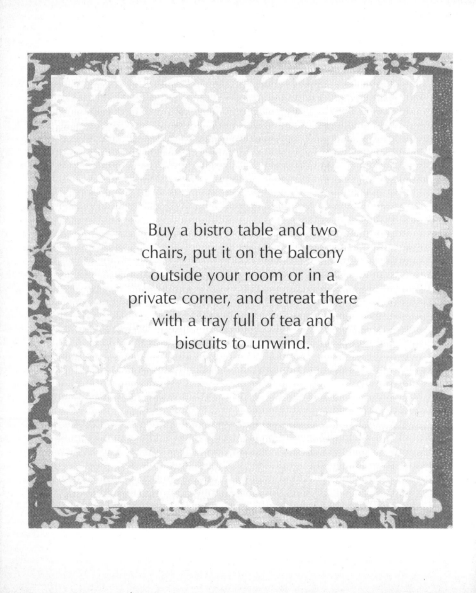

Buy a bistro table and two chairs, put it on the balcony outside your room or in a private corner, and retreat there with a tray full of tea and biscuits to unwind.

Buy something that calls out
your name in a store, even
though you have no practical
use for it. If it is pretty and you
like it, treat yourself.

"I never put off till tomorrow
what I can do the day after."

—Oscar Wilde

teal a chocolate moment. On a winter day, curl up in your flannel jammies with a cup of hot chocolate and a clipboard, and write down a story idea. Some of the best stories start out as a series of scribbles dotted with drizzles of hot chocolate.

*ind a quiet corner and
flip through your own baby
pictures and enjoy the
memories of your childhood.*

Buy a tape of your favorite
nature sounds—the ocean,
birds, the wind—and play it
softly as you fall asleep.

Go to a concert that strikes your fancy—jazz, country and western—whatever you love. Sing along, clap to the beat, and get lost in the music.

Garlands aren't just for Christmas. Your local craft store carries flower garlands in an array of colors and types. Use one to liven up your living room mantel or doorframe.

Tired of kids whining about dinner menus? Put up a large calendar and let each child pick a day and write in his favorite dish. Then follow these menu ideas, as wacky as they may be.

Beat the summer heat. Take a cool shower, spray on a light body cologne, and wear a gauzy dress around the house.

"There's a time when you have to explain to your children why they're born, and it's a marvelous thing if you know the reason by then."

—Hazel Scott

Meet a girlfriend at the
park *without* the kids—walk
around, splash in the fountains,
buy ice cream cones, and lie
on the grass.

Celebrate the fall weather. Gather a handful of autumn leaves and iron the loveliest between two sheets of waxed paper. Cut the leaves into your favorite shapes and tape them to the window in your bathroom.

*T*oo hot to garden? Put on your bathing suit and some sunblock, turn on the sprinkler, and pull weeds while you're getting sprayed.

Beat the winter chill with a little bit of fun. Fill your tub with hot water and lots of bubbles, turn on the music, and have a spa day.

Give yourself a pedicure, use a loofah to get rid of dead skin, paint your nails, and pluck your eyebrows. When you're done, wrap up in a terrycloth robe and pad around the house.

Hands-free accessories:
One of the best investments a
new mom can make is a Snugli
or other baby carrier. Strap that
baby onto your back and move!
Walk, clean, go to a museum,
shop . . . the baby will enjoy
the ride and you get to move!

Buy yourself a beautifully illustrated book of paper dolls (the queens of England, or the First Ladies). Cut them out and dress your dolls—just for fun!

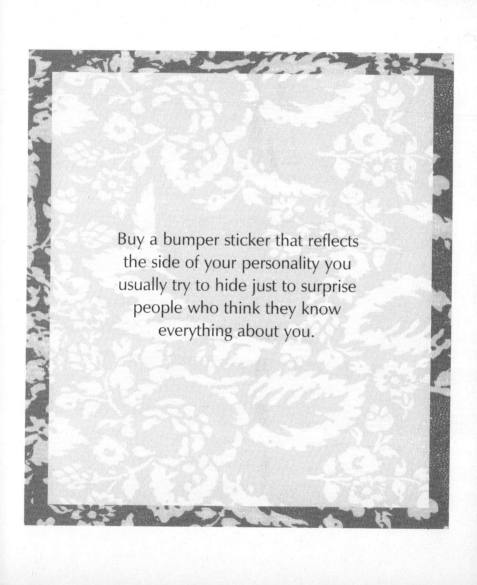

Buy a bumper sticker that reflects the side of your personality you usually try to hide just to surprise people who think they know everything about you.

Have a picnic all by yourself!
Stop by the deli section of
an upscale grocer and buy
individual servings of shrimp
salad, Brie, fancy crackers,
and éclairs.

"And in the end, it's not the years in your life that count. It's the life in your years."

—Abraham Lincoln

Safe sex? Science says that sexual fantasies can improve mood, reduce worry and tension, and minimize boredom. Take a walk on the wild side once in a while—in your imagination, that is . . .

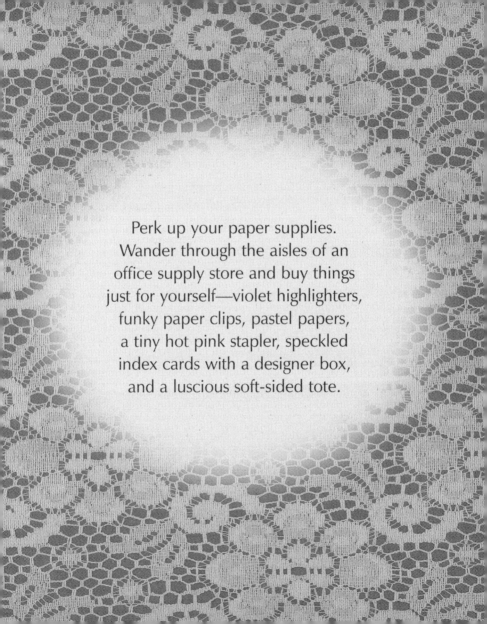

Perk up your paper supplies.
Wander through the aisles of an
office supply store and buy things
just for yourself—violet highlighters,
funky paper clips, pastel papers,
a tiny hot pink stapler, speckled
index cards with a designer box,
and a luscious soft-sided tote.

Go to your local coffee house, order a tall double-shot iced white mocha and sip it slowly at one of those cute little outdoor tables.

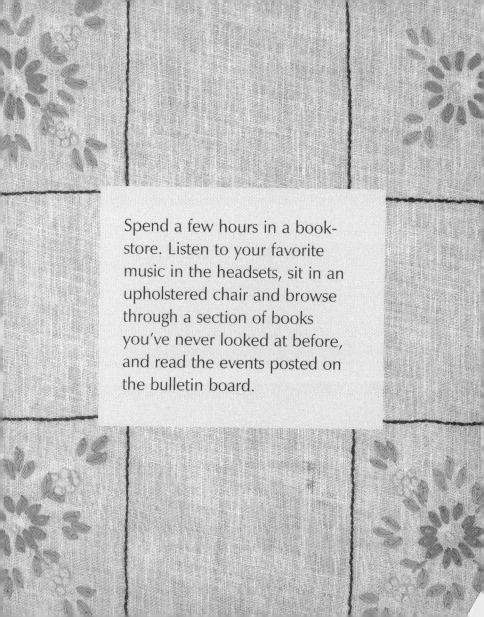

Spend a few hours in a book-
store. Listen to your favorite
music in the headsets, sit in an
upholstered chair and browse
through a section of books
you've never looked at before,
and read the events posted on
the bulletin board.

Make bookmarks for your friends with silk flowers, ribbons, stamps, whimsical buttons, and stickers—cover them with self-laminating paper and cut out the edges with scalloped scissors.

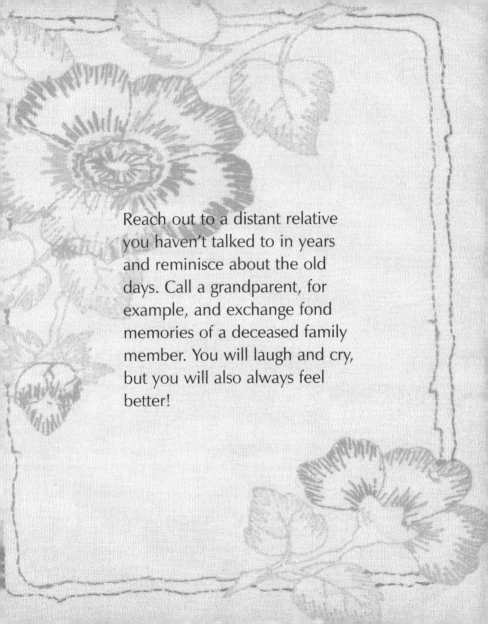

Reach out to a distant relative you haven't talked to in years and reminisce about the old days. Call a grandparent, for example, and exchange fond memories of a deceased family member. You will laugh and cry, but you will also always feel better!

*G*o to a discount Web site (Amazon.com's marketplace, or eBay's half.com) and browse for cheap used copies of your favorite old movies—*Beaches, Ghost, Coal Miner's Daughter, Love Story*. Buy a stock to watch when you're alone.

Embrace your inner "artiste." Grab your digital camera and take photographs of fun things— flower blossoms, grapevines, autumn leaves, luscious desserts at the bakery, sailboats on the lake. Or enlarge and crop small sections of your photos to result in an unidentifiable image and voilá . . . instant modern art!

"*Peace is always beautiful.*"

—*Walt Whitman*

Get out an old handwritten recipe from your mother or grandmother and make it just for fun. Serve it that evening with a photo of your loved one in a beautiful frame in the center of the table.

Have a spa day with your daughters—long soaks in the tub with lots of bubbles and loofahs, massages, manicures and pedicures, and fancy hairdos with hot rollers. Serve "wine" (grape juice) and "coffee" (hot chocolate) along with baskets of fruit and fancy cookies, just like the real spas.

Buy a tiny Christmas tree just for yourself, and decorate it just the way you like it—use your heirloom ornaments, or buy a few new ones just for fun.

Get in the holiday spirit. Go to a craft store and buy a Christmas wreath, white spray-on snow, and lots of small fancy Christmas decorations. Back at home, turn on Christmas carols and make a wreath to hang in your bedroom.

$\mathcal{F}$ingerpaints aren't just for the kids—let your fingers do the walking and create something special.

Brighten up a dull corner with a new gallery of art! Gather some of the best artwork you've been collecting from your kids, take it to a craft store, and select mats or frames that provide the perfect complement.

*G*o online and look up one of your best friends from high school—then send an e-mail or call to reminisce about old times.

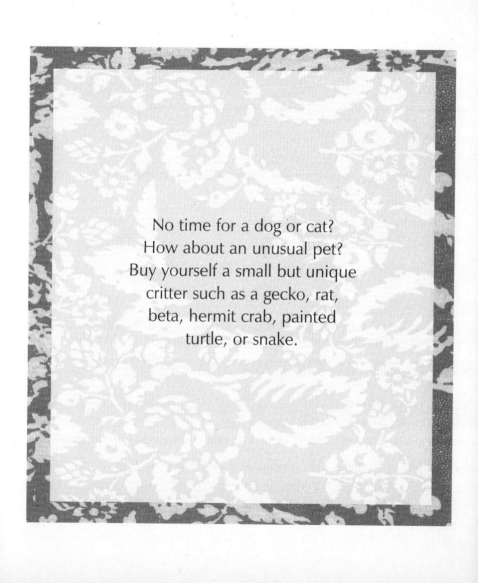

No time for a dog or cat?
How about an unusual pet?
Buy yourself a small but unique
critter such as a gecko, rat,
beta, hermit crab, painted
turtle, or snake.

Invite a couple of girlfriends over for a pajama party—flannel robes, old videos, popcorn, a warm fire, and sleeping bags.

"Those who dream by day are cognizant of many things which escape those who dream only by night."

—Edgar Allan Poe

Set up the tent in the backyard
for the kids, then enjoy having
the family room to yourself and
indulge in some old movies.

Set up the tent in the backyard
for yourself! Have a spontaneous
sleep-out with your partner or
on your own.

Having trouble falling asleep? Chamomile tea with a bit of honey will soothe and calm.

Take a trip to the mall or outlet
stores and gather some great
bargains for Christmas
(so what if it's only March?).

When a friend has a tough decision to make, remember that the kindest and truest thing you can say is that you will stick by her whatever she decides— and mean it!

*N*o matter how long your list of things you need to do for others, remember to put yourself at the top of that list and do something nice for yourself first.

Make sure your daily vocabulary
is filled with words of praise for
those close to you, especially your
children. Phrases like "you are so
strong," "you are so smart," and
"how brave of you to do that"
mean more than you know.

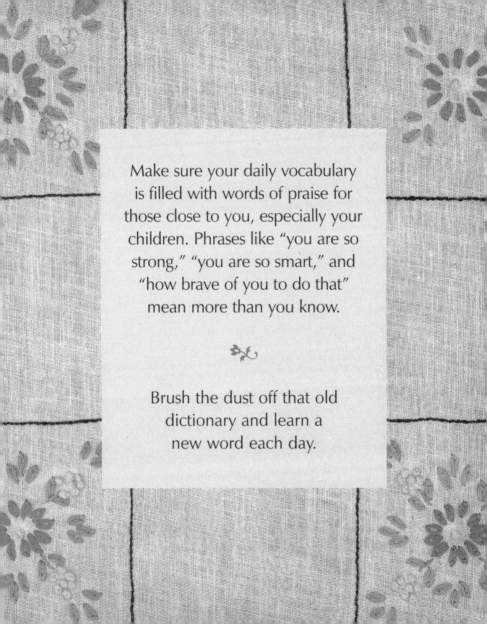

Brush the dust off that old
dictionary and learn a
new word each day.

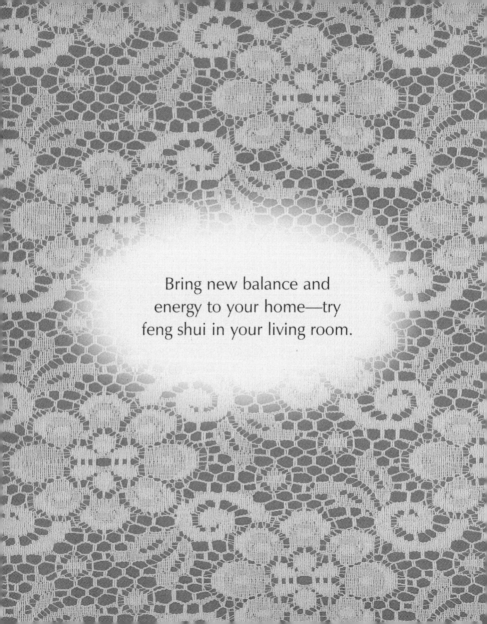

Bring new balance and
energy to your home—try
feng shui in your living room.

Go for an evening cruise in your car. Roll down the windows, feel the wind in your hair, and sing along to your favorite tunes!

Things are never really
as bad as they feel.

"There are two ways to live your life. One is as though nothing is a miracle. The other is as though everything is a miracle."

—Albert Einstein

A great bumper sticker
for positive expression?
"Expect a Miracle"

*T*ape-record yourself reading your children's favorite books and give it to them. No matter how old they are now, they will treasure the tape. They can listen to it when they are blue or even play it for their own kids when they have them.

*I*f you have trouble falling asleep some night, play that tape of the children's book for yourself. Nothing is as soothing as the rhythmic lines of a children's classic. The story will bring up good memories and help lull you to sleep.

When your child is away
at camp or college, send a
care package with his favorite
home-baked cookies and
other special keepsakes to
remind him of home.

Ask your son or daughter
to teach you to play a sport
you never played, and then
join him or her for a game.

*G*et your kids to organize a
concert for you; then sit back
with a big bowl of popcorn
and enjoy the show.

Every day is a new opportunity for growth. Expand your mind. Take an evening course, read a book on a new subject, try something new like yoga or pilates, or join a book club.

When you feel like your life is just a long to-do list, take a dance break. Turn up the music and boogie until you feel the clouds lift.

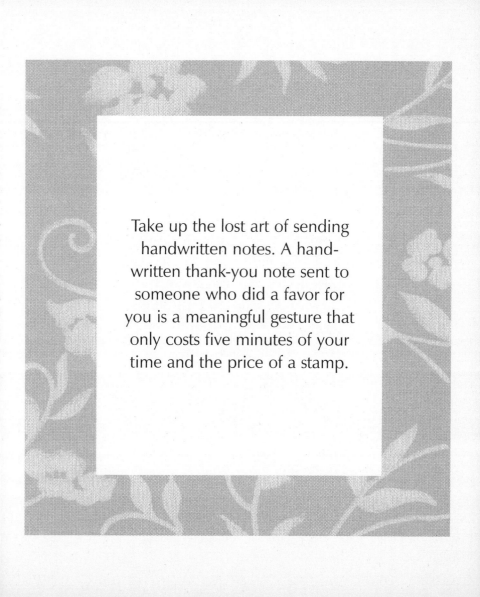

Take up the lost art of sending handwritten notes. A handwritten thank-you note sent to someone who did a favor for you is a meaningful gesture that only costs five minutes of your time and the price of a stamp.

Tip the counter person at the doughnut shop, the gas station attendant, the bagger at the market—a smile and a dollar to show your appreciation will make their day.

Sneak away some weekday
afternoon by yourself and go
catch a movie you have been
wanting to see.

Create a sanctuary in your own home—claim a corner and stock it with your favorite things— fluffy pillows, comfy throws, and favorite books. Enjoy quiet moments for yourself.

*"One should always be
a little improbable."*

—Oscar Wilde

Don't use warm snuggly beds and pajamas just when you are sick! Take a pajama day for yourself. Keep your favorite pajamas on, take a tray with coffee and cinnamon toast into your room, and lounge in bed reading a good book.

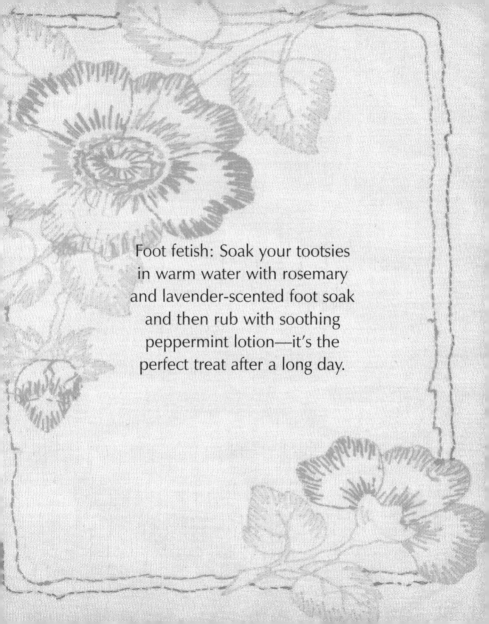

Foot fetish: Soak your tootsies in warm water with rosemary and lavender-scented foot soak and then rub with soothing peppermint lotion—it's the perfect treat after a long day.

*I*f you love candles, create candle landscapes. Use sand, seashells, colorful beads, river rocks, beach glass, and other colorful natural items spread out on large ceramic plates or pottery. Different colored candles of various shapes and sizes finish off the design.

Dim the lights. Candles are not just for power outages. Light them and let the soft glow become part of your daily ritual!

"The man who views the
world at fifty the same way
he did at twenty has wasted
thirty years of his life."

—Muhammad Ali

Bring some variety to
your fitness routine by taking
a dance fitness class such as
swinging cardio, hip-hop, or
yoga ballet. Break a sweat
and have fun doing it!

Relieve tension and aid relaxation by trying foot massage. Convince your partner to give it a try. You can buy reflexology socks with color-coded symbols on the soles demonstrating the corresponding body parts.

"My idea of superwoman
is someone who scrubs
her own floors."

—Bette Midler

"I never make an important decision before I nap."

—*Winston Churchill*

Like to nap? A recent medical study lends credence to Churchill's nap habit by claiming that a nap of any length does the body and the brain good. So the next time you feel the desire to take a nap, don't feel guilty—your brain needs the nap in order to work better!

De-stress after a long day. Lock the bathroom door and fill up the tub with lavender oil and bubble bath. Soak until your muscles are completely relaxed. Follow up with a salt scrub and loofah until your skin tingles. Smooth a fragrant body lotion all over and put on your softest cotton lounging clothes. Finish with ten minutes of deep breathing exercises and a soothing CD.

The Web site *www.fitday.com* is a free online journal and exercise log you can use to keep track of your daily diet and exercise routine. In addition to helping you calculate the fat grams and calories of what you eat each day, the site helps you monitor your daily progress by recording your thoughts and activities.

*T*ry paying your bills online—it makes your life just a little bit easier. Every little bit helps when you have so much to do!

*"Life is a great bundle
of little things."*

—*Oliver Wendell Holmes*

There is no such thing as a
mistake. Every action, every
situation is just another
opportunity to learn.

A guiding principle: Each and every day, do only those things that will enable you to feel good about yourself later.

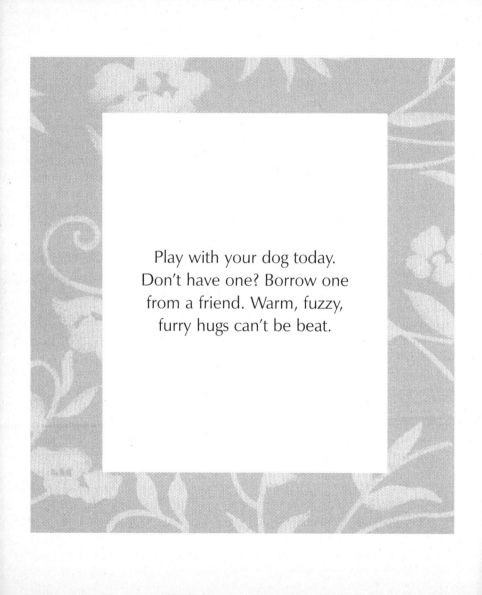

Play with your dog today. Don't have one? Borrow one from a friend. Warm, fuzzy, furry hugs can't be beat.

Never underestimate the
power of a good walk
to make you feel better.

Treat yourself to a bowl of your favorite childhood cereal. Coco Puffs, Lucky Charms, or Sugar Smacks—whatever your heart's desire—eat a big bowl and enjoy it without guilt.

The next time a saleswoman tries to give you a free makeover at the Lancôme counter at Macy's, let her. You really are not obligated to buy anything more than a lipstick and you get to look great for a day.

Kitchen Shortcut

Quick Hummus Wrap

Put 1 can of drained chickpeas in a blender or processor. Add 2 peeled cloves of garlic, juice of half a lemon, half a bunch of fresh parsley leaves, ¼ cup of olive oil, a dash of Tabasco, and 1 tablespoon of toasted sesame seeds. Blend till mixed and creamy. Roll in a whole-wheat wrap and enjoy.

"If you bungle raising your children, I don't think whatever else you do matters very much."

—Jacqueline Kennedy Onassis

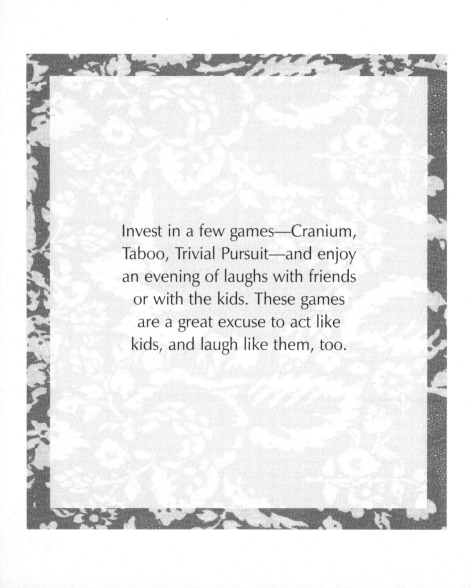

Invest in a few games—Cranium, Taboo, Trivial Pursuit—and enjoy an evening of laughs with friends or with the kids. These games are a great excuse to act like kids, and laugh like them, too.

Pep up your wardrobe with some bold-colored clothing as a change from the usual browns and blacks. A fuchsia blouse, a lime green T-shirt, pastel pink capris, and even a brightly colored scarf will show everyone you are confident and willing to take a risk. You might be surprised to find out how many outfits go with red leather boots!

Here's an easy relaxation exercise: Grab five minutes when you can be alone and sit in a relaxed position with your head and shoulders loose.

Clear your mind of all random thoughts and go to your favorite place. Whether it is a patch of grass under a weeping willow tree, a spot of beach with the waves rolling in, or a cozy couch in front of a roaring fire, imagine yourself in your favorite place free of all worries, pressures, and responsibilities for at least five minutes.

Afterward, go and face the rest of the day with renewed energy and calm.

*N*ever underestimate the power of a smile. Studies have shown that smiling boosts serotonin levels, making you feel good even when you don't. So, create your own happiness by smiling, even when you feel low.

Who says your workspace has to be dull? Spice up your desk with fun items such as a wind-up toy, a Zen sand garden, a stress ball, crossword dice, bright flowers, a jar of Jelly Bellys— you get the idea . . .

The next time your best friend's birthday comes around, show her you care by putting a little extra effort into the birthday message. Plan it so that she gets a different birthday card in the mail every day for the six days surrounding her actual birthday, three before and three after.

List ten things you like about yourself. Then, just when you think you are done, list ten more and don't stop until you are done. Then, post it on your bathroom mirror and read it every morning.

*S*end flowers to your
mother on *your* birthday.
She'll get the message.

Cash in that coin jar you have been slowly filling. Take it to the automated coin sorter that most supermarkets have near the registers and dump in the collection. Collect your cash and go to the nearest Bath & Body Works and splurge on luxury spa items.

*L*ock yourself in the bath-room with a few scented candles and soak in lavender-vanilla bath foam.

Scrub your skin with a peppermint or grapefruit sugar scrub and purify your complexion with a Dead Sea mud mask. Finish off by moisturizing with eucalyptus-spearmint massage oil and Shea cream for your feet.

When you are done, drop a few quarters in your coin jar and start your spa savings account all over again!

Taste the memories of your childhood by making yourself a root beer float or an authentic Brooklyn-style egg cream.

"Cleaning your house while
the kids are still growing is
like shoveling the walk before
it stops snowing."

—Phyllis Diller

Read your favorite book from your young adult days. The entire Tolkien trilogy, *The Mists of Avalon*, *Great Expectations*, or *Light a Penny Candle*—whatever your favorite was, take it off the shelf, dust it off, and re-enter that wonderful world.

Better yet, read it aloud a little bit at a time to your partner or loved one each night before bed. Not only do you get to rediscover your favorite book, you get to share it with someone you love.

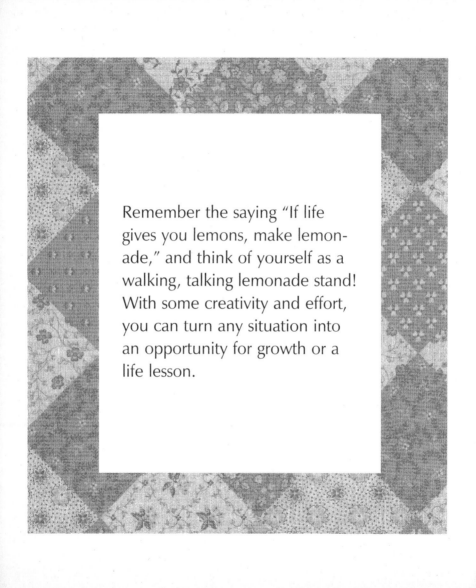

Remember the saying "If life gives you lemons, make lemonade," and think of yourself as a walking, talking lemonade stand! With some creativity and effort, you can turn any situation into an opportunity for growth or a life lesson.

*B*ake a cake for someone special
and decorate it with a smiley
face or a message of love. Don't
wait for a special occasion—do
it on any old day.

Having difficulty parting with old or unused items around the house? Use this rule of thumb: If you have not used it for more than a year, toss it. The consolation? Getting rid of old things makes it possible for new and better things to enter your living space.

Faced with a tough decision?
Ask yourself what your life would
look like a year from now if you
take one course or the other.
Projecting the event forward
might give you some insight into
the better choice to make.

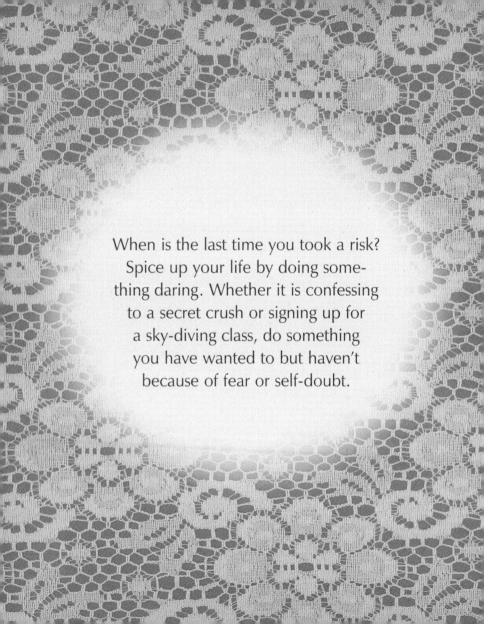

When is the last time you took a risk?
Spice up your life by doing something daring. Whether it is confessing
to a secret crush or signing up for
a sky-diving class, do something
you have wanted to but haven't
because of fear or self-doubt.

*C*hange your thoughts as if you're changing a CD you don't like. Yes, it's that easy. You *do* have a choice about how you react to situations. You can let the negative feelings overwhelm you, or you can choose to step outside yourself and think about how you want to react to any given situation.

*I*s someone you love down with the flu? Show your love by making a pot of homemade chicken soup from scratch. Enjoy sharing steaming cups of soup while you watch a funny movie together.

Kitchen Shortcut

Homemade chicken noodle soup is easier to make than you may think and so much more nurturing than buying the canned version from the store. A surprisingly good shortcut is to buy a small chicken and a "Soup Starter" packet. Add some fresh sliced carrots and a can of drained corn, and you end up with as close to homemade as possible in half the time.

*T*hink of the benefits of getting older. You are smarter, more experienced, and more self-aware than you were five or ten years ago . . . and that makes you more powerful. How you use that power is up to you.

"If you obey all the rules,
you miss all the fun."

—Katharine Hepburn

The next time it rains,
put on your galoshes
and jump in the puddles.

Take a walk in the rain
on a summer day.

Join a dance class one night a week. You will make friends, learn some new steps, and get in some fun, vigorous exercise while you do it!

Pick up three bouquets of daffodils—one for your desk, one for your home, and one for a coworker.

Eating alone? That's still no reason to gulp down your meal while standing at the kitchen counter. Pass on the paper plates and use your good china, crystal stemware, and linen napkins. Light a candle and enjoy your dinner peacefully.

New mom tip: Nap when the baby naps. Instead of rushing to complete all the tasks that could not be done while your arms were occupied holding the baby, do the one thing that you absolutely cannot do when he is awake—sleep!

Your bedroom is not the place to economize. Buy high thread-count cotton or sateen sheets, a good down comforter, plenty of fluffy pillows, and a quality mattress. Use scented linen spray each time you change the sheets and keep a supply of tealights by the bed for nighttime lighting.

Your bed should be a haven at the end of the day—a place you can go not only to rest, but to nurture and pamper yourself, and recharge your body and spirit for the next day.

Have a costume or theme party just for fun. Go all out with decorations and food tied to the theme. It will be an occasion you and your friends will remember.

Spend a fall afternoon raking leaves. If you don't have a yard, do it for a friend and you will be giving a gift while getting a gift. As you work, appreciate the sound of rustling leaves and the sight of the vivid colors.

When you say you're sorry for something, make sure you mean it. Think about all the times when your "I'm sorry" really meant "I'm sorry I got caught—now stop giving me grief about it."

Remember, the joy is in the journey. Take your time and experience the process instead of just focusing on the goal.

"Failure is just a way for our lives to show us we're moving in the wrong direction; that we should try something different."

—Oprah Winfrey

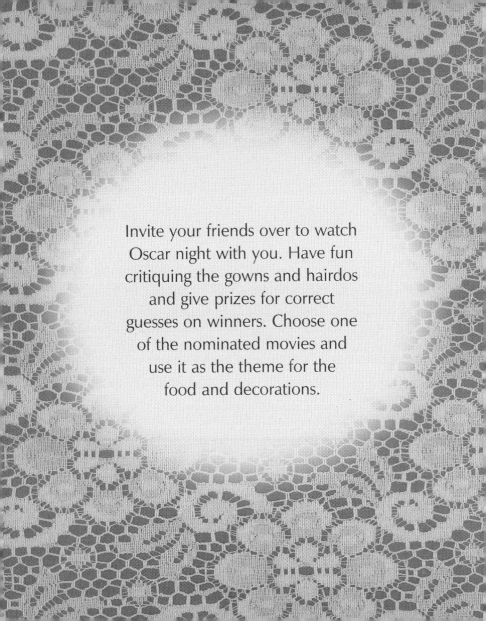

Invite your friends over to watch Oscar night with you. Have fun critiquing the gowns and hairdos and give prizes for correct guesses on winners. Choose one of the nominated movies and use it as the theme for the food and decorations.

The best things in life *are* free: a lazy Sunday afternoon; a walk on a deserted beach; newly fallen snow before dawn; holding someone you love by a crackling fire; playing fetch with your dog; a newborn baby; the list is endless . . .

Winter sports! Make snow angels on freshly fallen snow. Make a snowwoman in your front yard and dress her up with a plaid scarf and black beret. Have a snowball fight. Glide down a hill on a makeshift sled of flattened-out cardboard.

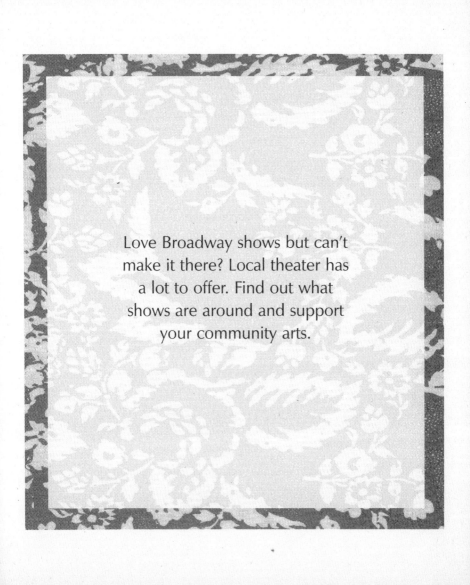

Love Broadway shows but can't make it there? Local theater has a lot to offer. Find out what shows are around and support your community arts.

*R*ediscover your faith. Attend
religious services if you can, but
at a minimum, discover the
peace of prayer and meditation.

Create your own "altar" or sacred space for your prayer and meditation time. Set up a small table surrounded by cushions on the floor. Put objects on the altar that have a special meaning for you—photos of loved ones, both living and gone; stones, sea-shells, and other objects from nature; your grandmother's rosary; you get the idea.

Finish off the area with can-dles; a water fountain; and a CD of meditative music, such as Gregorian chants or Enya, and you have the perfect setting for your quiet time to get in touch with your spiritual side.

Have you heard the saying, "Be a human being, not a human doing"? Think about what that really means. Can you slow down enough to stop focusing on what you have to get done and just "be" in each moment? You will enjoy your life more when you are actually *participating* in it instead of holding on for dear life as the days fly by.

Have a '70s party. Play disco music and dress up in '70s-style clothing. Dust off those mood rings, bell-bottoms, and stacked heels, and hang up a rotating disco ball from a party store. Encourage the guys to play too and dress like Travolta and you'll be all set for a "hustle" down memory lane.

Go to a poetry reading.

Write poetry. It's easier than
you think and a great creative
exercise for getting in touch
with your feelings.

Have your own poetry reading. Invite friends and serve lattes. Buy a book of poetry (try the *Nine Horses* by Billy Collins, U.S. poet laureate) and read it out loud to guests. Finish with an "open mike" and encourage friends to come up and read their own poetry. Be brave and break the ice by reading yours first!

"It's like magic. When you live by yourself, all your annoying habits are gone!"

—*Merrill Markoe*

If you are single, learn to appreciate your solitary state. If you persist in thinking that being single is a temporary condition you need to remedy, you will always feel like something is wrong with your life.

"It is true that I never should have married, but I didn't want to live without a man. Brought up to respect the conventions, love had to end in marriage. I'm afraid it did."

—Bette Davis, *The Lonely Life*, 1962

Go to a local auction. Have fun by bidding on items within your budget. Don't be afraid to buy a piece of furniture as a makeover project for a rainy day. Imagine that $5 diamond-in-the-rough with a good sanding and a paint job!

Have a friend with a convertible? Have a nighttime adventure. Put the top down and take a drive into the countryside or up a mountain road. Pull over, put your head back, and stargaze.

*B*reathe. Some believe that holding one's breath is a way to keep down feelings. The next time you're in a stressful or anxious situation, stop a moment and pay attention to your breath. Take a few belly-deep breaths, fill your diaphragm, and let it out. You might be surprised at the flood of feelings that comes to the surface.

*A*n incontrovertible truth is that feelings are not facts. Just because you feel fear does not necessarily mean that a dangerous situation exists. Acknowledge uncomfortable feelings for what they are and let them pass through and out of you.

Adopt the practice of saying grace before meals. Regardless of your particular beliefs, a quiet moment to acknowledge life's gifts and express gratitude for the little things (such as homecooked meals) can only lift your spirits and improve your day.

Commit to a nightly ritual of prayer. Your prayer can be a simple action, such as pausing to say thank-you to the universe for another good day before jumping into bed, or you can have a more formal practice of kneeling or sitting yoga-style by your altar for longer prayers and meditation to end your day. Either way, the connection to your higher power is the point and just doing it will give you much-needed serenity.

Kitchen Shortcut

Quick Lavash Pizzas

Easy to make and serve, these lavash bread pizzas have a thin crispy crust that is a perfect bed for melted cheese and fresh vegetables. Vary by using mozzarella or Cheddar cheese, or making it Mexican with olives, salsa, and sour cream.

1 package of lavash square bread
Good-quality olive oil
Various sliced fresh veggies such
    as very thinly sliced onions,
    peppers, mushrooms,
    zucchini, tomatoes, and garlic

1 container of feta cheese
   crumbles

Place two of the lavash breads flat on
the counter. Drizzle olive oil over the
bread and then spread a layer of sliced
veggies over the oil. Crumble feta
cheese over the top of the vegetables
and give it another small drizzle of oil.
Place the breads into a 325-degree
preheated oven for 15 minutes.

"She discovered with great delight that one does not love one's children just because they are one's children but because of the friendship formed while raising them."

—Gabriel Garcia Marquez,
Love in the Time of Cholera

reate a gift your child will treasure forever. Keep a journal for your children as they grow and give it to them when they are adults. At least once or twice a year, write a long letter in the journal addressed to your child. Recount the special moments as well as the ordinary.

Remember hopscotch? Draw a hopscotch grid on your driveway or sidewalk with colored chalk and go for it!

Buy a bucket of sidewalk
chalk and express yourself!

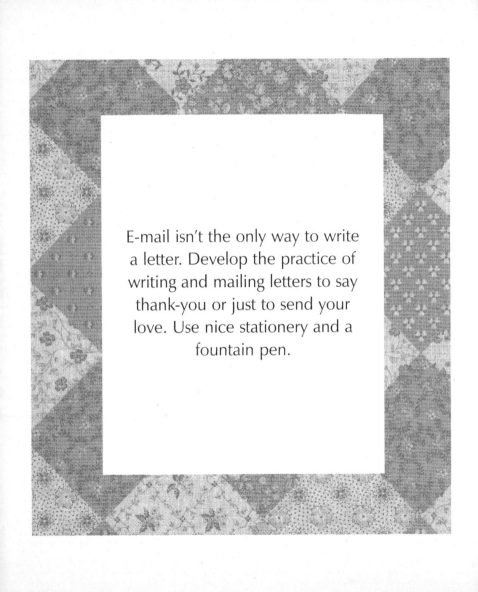

E-mail isn't the only way to write a letter. Develop the practice of writing and mailing letters to say thank-you or just to send your love. Use nice stationery and a fountain pen.

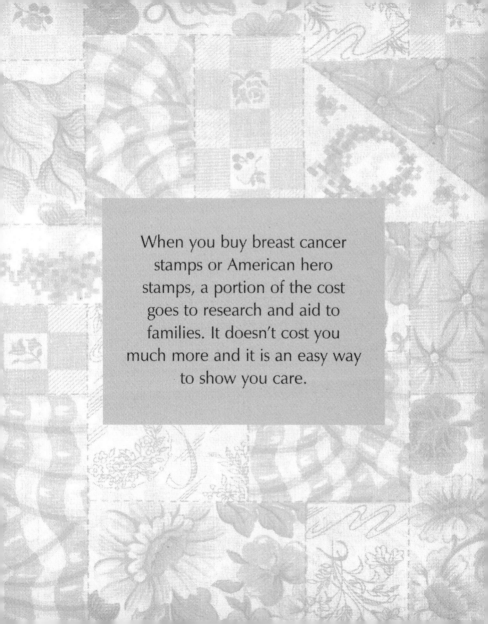

When you buy breast cancer stamps or American hero stamps, a portion of the cost goes to research and aid to families. It doesn't cost you much more and it is an easy way to show you care.

Awareness is the first step
toward change. Is there
something about yourself or
your life that you would like
to change?

Sometimes happiness comes when we least expect it and in the most surprising ways. Keep your eyes open for the surprise.

Have you heard the saying, "When one door closes, another one opens"? Close the door firmly on what is over and don't look back. Move forward to the new possibilities in store for you.

The other part of that saying goes: "When one door closes, another opens, *but the hallway is a painful place to be!*" During times of transition, remember that the discomfort is temporary.

"*Don't look back—
you're not going that way!*"

—*Mary Engelbreit*

Get into the "swing" of things—
what's better than a hammock,
your favorite book, and the
shade of a big oak tree?

Buy yourself some of your favorite childhood candy and have a party with yourself. Don't forget the candy necklaces, Pixie Stix, Bazooka bubble gum, M&Ms, candy cigarettes, and Whoppers.

Learn a poem by heart.

Take a few seconds to make your bed in the morning. The payoff is wonderful: coming home to a neat room after work.

Grab a bench at the mall and people-watch with a friend. It's fun to observe the different people, their clothes, and their behavior. Make up stories about what they are doing and where they are going.

*T*reat yourself and a friend to an authentic Japanese meal in a tatami room. Take off your shoes, sit on cushions on the floor, eat with chopsticks, and don't forget to try the sushi.

*W*ander around a museum on a rainy day. Pick one painting as your "own" and imagine where you would put it in your house. Visit it often.

Make an old-fashioned banana split in an ice cream dish. Top it off with whipped cream and walnuts. Don't forget the cherry!

When was the last time you played an April Fool's Day prank on someone? Rediscover your sense of humor and have some harmless fun with your friends, family members, and coworkers next April 1st.

Skin care does not have to be expensive. Mix half a mashed banana, half a ripe mashed avocado, and ¼ cup oatmeal in a bowl for a fantastic moisturizing facial.

*"Give to the world the best
you have, and the best will
come back to you."*

—*Madeline Bridge*

Remember that what goes
around comes around. Look
for opportunities to be kind
and feel the results.

Get down on the ground and play jacks or pickup sticks with your daughter and her friends.

Beat February cabin fever by hosting a beach party. Fill a couple of cheap kiddie pools with sand and sand toys, but reserve one for bags of ice and beer!

Put out your beach chairs and beach towels for seating, break out the summer clothes and sunglasses, and put the Beach Boys on the CD player.

Don't forget that limbo stick. Hang up colorful beach lanterns and invite your friends over for a summer blast they will really appreciate.

Do the karaoke thing. Go to a karaoke bar with your friends and pick an old favorite and belt it out for the crowd.

$\mathcal{T}$hink about saving the life of a puppy or kitten at the pound. You will be giving the gift of life as you give yourself the gift of a true companion that will give you love and loyalty forever.

Throw a "clothes exchange" party with your friends. Have them bring clothes and accessories they don't wear anymore or are tired of. Try on each other's outfits and have an impromptu fashion show. You and your friends get to shop for free and have a lot of laughs while you do it.

Have you made
your gratitude list today?

*T*reat yourself and a special friend to a night out on the town. Pick a fancy restaurant and a Broadway show, and rent a limo. Pick up the tab for the whole evening and make it a surprise. You will feel great and so will your guest.

Find out about local chapters of the Special Olympics or Habitat for Humanity, and lend a helping hand to those in need.

$\mathcal{L}$earn to tango. There is no hotter dance to do with your lover.

Expand your mind.
Listen to public radio for
a change instead of music.

"When you are a mother, you are never really alone in your thoughts. A mother always has to think twice, once for herself and once for her child."

—Sophia Loren

Go "yard sailing." Choose one weekend morning, grab a friend and the classifieds, and map out a route to hit all the garage and yard sales in the area.

During the next big snowstorm, turn out all the lights in your living room and open the curtains wide. Lie back and watch the swirling snowflakes against the black night sky.

*T*hink about this: Do you have one friend you can call any time of the night or day? A friend who would take your call at 3:00 A.M. and stay on the phone and talk you through whatever anxiety you're having? If so, then treasure that friend and keep her close.

Then, think about this:
Are you that kind of friend
to at least one person?

If you're always the one in aerobics class who is lifting the right leg while everyone else is lifting the left, join a water aerobics class. Not only is it great exercise, but nobody can see what you're moving or not moving underwater!

Enjoy a spring afternoon with a picnic. Spread a blanket under a weeping willow tree and enjoy the sights, smells, and sounds all around you. All you need is a basket with fresh fruit, bread and cheese, a bottle of iced tea, and your favorite book.

Go apple picking in the fall and bring home a big basket of apples. Make homemade applesauce and apple pies. Pile apples in a big wooden bowl in the center of your dining room table.

In the summer, go to a strawberry field and pick baskets of fresh strawberries. Make homemade strawberry jam, strawberry shortcakes with fresh whipped cream, and a fresh fruit tart. Put some in a freezer bag for another time.

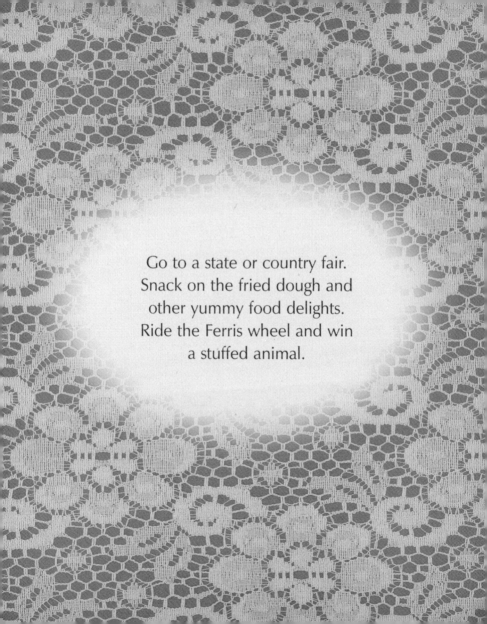

Go to a state or country fair.
Snack on the fried dough and
other yummy food delights.
Ride the Ferris wheel and win
a stuffed animal.

*"'I can't help it'... that's what
we all say when we don't want
to exert ourselves."*

—*Eva Lathbury*

*I*f we don't take responsibility for anything, then nobody can blame us when things go wrong. But being passive cheats us of the exhilaration and excitement that comes with accomplishment! You will never fulfill your potential by playing it safe; or, as the old saying goes, "Nothing ventured, nothing gained!"

*Wintertime ideas
for your home*

When it's time to decorate for
the winter holidays, take a ride
in the countryside and clip some
fresh pine and evergreen
boughs. You'll love the scent,
and it's a creative change from
an artificial garland.

Spice up your holiday table with
a basket of fresh pine cones and
cinnamon sticks.

Add a touch of old-fashioned charm to your tree this year by stringing popcorn and cranberries.

Make hot mulled cider with spices and cinnamon sticks and simmer it in the slow cooker all afternoon, roast some chestnuts, and play your favorite holiday album.

Lights aren't only for your Christmas tree! String some over your doorways, along your mantel, or on that ficus tree in the corner for an extra-festive glow.

Family photo albums shouldn't sit on a shelf collecting dust. Sit with your children, young or grown, and reminisce as you turn the pages. Tell the stories of the pictures over and over again. You will be building memories for young children and reinforcing the memories for the grown.

For a Sunday morning treat,
bake blueberry muffins with
real blueberries—the smell
alone is worth it!

Play hooky. Call in sick and
spend the day doing absolutely
nothing constructive.

The next time you're out shopping and you see that perfect dress, try it on, even if you're not going to buy it!

Host a scary movie night. Rent *The Exorcist, Signs, The Blair Witch Project, The Ring, Sixth Sense, Darkness Falls*, and other fright classics. Don't be too shy to scream out loud at the scary parts—that's half the fun!

"She had trouble defining herself independently of her husband, tried to talk to him about it, but he said nonsense, he had no trouble defining her at all."

—Cynthia Propper Seton

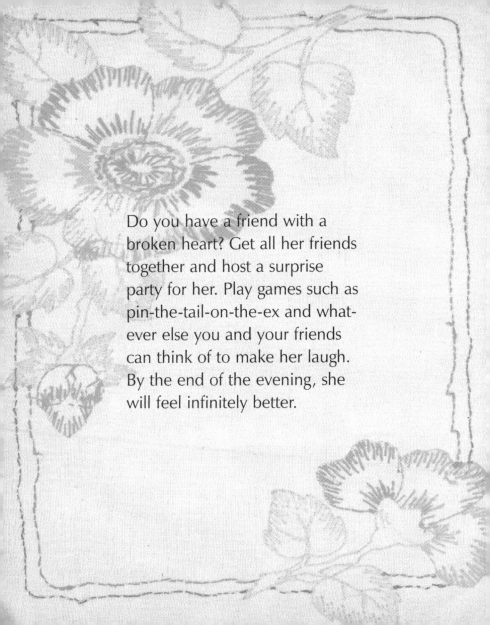

Do you have a friend with a broken heart? Get all her friends together and host a surprise party for her. Play games such as pin-the-tail-on-the-ex and whatever else you and your friends can think of to make her laugh. By the end of the evening, she will feel infinitely better.

*B*uy Girl Scout cookies
and enjoy them with a
glass of cold milk.

Catch a sunset. Sit in the grass
and watch the fantastic colors
splash across the sky.

When was the last time you rode a roller coaster? Share the thrill: Find a big one and ride it with someone special. Hold on to each other tightly and scream as loud as you want to.

Does your home need a makeover? Pick some daring colors and have a painting party. Let your friends help you redecorate and don't be afraid to try something new and fun!

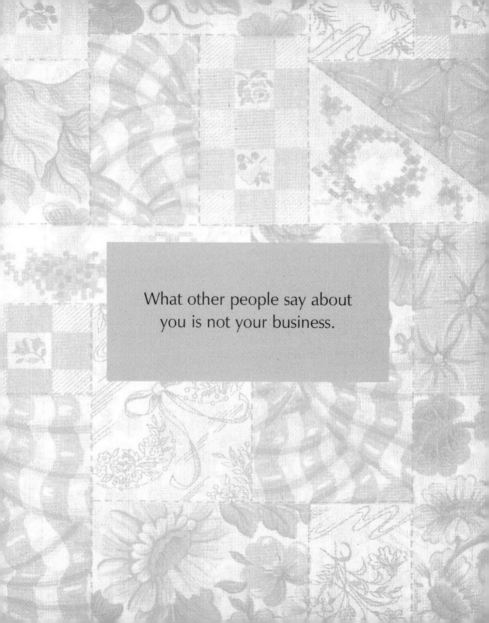

What other people say about
you is not your business.

Post this saying on your desk at work: "The people who matter don't mind; the people who mind don't matter."

*B*usy schedule? Make sure you set aside one-on-one time for your children and partner. Whether you walk together, read together, play games with each other, or even just nap together, the time you spend together is important and should always be a priority.

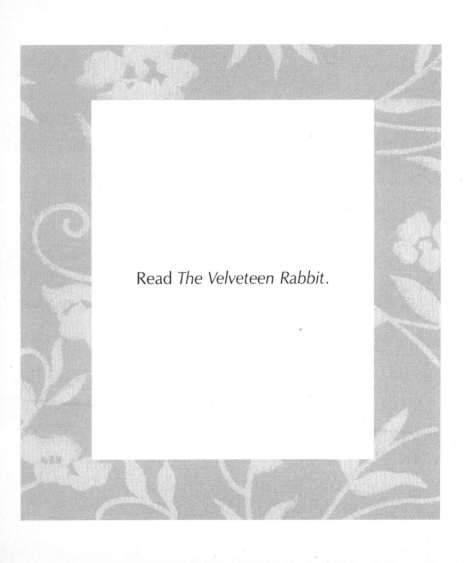

Read *The Velveteen Rabbit*.

Try some aromatherapy. Bowls of potpourri add fabulous scents to your home and office.

Scented linen sprays add a hint of springtime to your sheets and won't stain your fabrics. Buy one in your favorite scent.

On your feet all day? Try a spritz of peppermint foot spray to re-energize tired tootsies.

Ask for a foot massage. Promise to return the favor.

Fresh face: For toning and refreshment, try a lemon astringent in your morning beauty routine.

"Life is either a daring adventure or nothing."

—*Helen Keller*

The choice is yours to make each and every moment: to participate fully in this thing called "life" or to withdraw, pull inward, and let life happen to you. Which choice will you make?

When you love someone, you want to see her achieve her highest potential, to be the best person she can possibly be. Sometimes, to honor that might mean you have to give up something you want for yourself. Do it quietly, and without the need for recognition or fanfare.

Ask your partner to brush your
hair. Relax with each stroke.

Late sleeper? Get up early.

Early riser? Stay in bed for
a few extra minutes.

*"You must do the thing you
think you cannot do."*

—*Eleanor Roosevelt*

Fill your workspace with bright and beautiful objects that make you happy

Color me creative? Splashes of unexpected colors can be a welcome change from the obligatory office gray. The principles of feng shui say that brilliant colors like scarlet and lemon yellow can spur creativity, boost confidence, and lift your mood.

Toss a hand-crocheted shawl over your office chair for days when the air conditioner is too strong.

Natural colors and textures will warm things up—a sisal grass in-box, a bowl of dried flower petals, a walnut-finished fountain pen, an amethyst paperweight—these touches of nature are much-needed reminders of the outdoors during long stretches in the office.

Surround your workspace with items that have strong personal associations for you to keep you connected during those times you feel like an anonymous employee. Display framed family photos, write with your grandmother's antique fountain pen to jot notes, or use your dad's worn pocketwatch as a paperweight.

"*Proceed* as the way opens" is a saying said to be of Quaker origin. Whenever you think you may be forcing something or trying to control the outcome of a situation, pause, take a deep breath, think about the wisdom of these words, and loosen your grip . . .

"Noble deeds and hot
baths are the best cures
for depression."

—Dodie Smith

Peace of mind

True peace of mind comes from
knowing the difference between
what you can change and what
you should accept.

Everything is exactly the way it is
supposed to be . . . true peace
of mind comes from believing
this statement.

The level of one's serenity is directly proportionate to the level of acceptance one has about any given situation.

Without life's pain, one would never recognize the value of contentment.

Sometimes all you can do is put one foot in front of the other. And, if all you can do is take a baby step, then that is better than not taking any action at all.

"My formula for living is quite simple. I get up in the morning and I go to bed at night. In between I occupy myself as best I can."

—Cary Grant

A friend indeed . . .

Spend some time with a good
friend. A good friend is someone
who can sit with you on cold
winter nights in complete silence
and not be uncomfortable. She is
capable of just being there for
you without feeling like she has
to say the right thing or have all
the answers.

A friend accepts you for who
you are and believes in you,
sometimes even despite evi-
dence to the contrary . . .

Take the trouble to tell someone just how much her friendship means to you.

If you are lucky enough to be on the receiving end of good friend-ships, make sure you are giving back. Imagine the very best friend a person could have, then become that friend yourself to someone new in your life.

Can you be 100 percent gen-uinely happy for someone else's good fortune? If you can, then you have earned the title of true friend to that person.

Try your own home version of the river stone massage given in the best spas.

Choose rocks of various sizes with smooth surfaces. Wash them and then rub them with sesame or lavender oil. Fill your slow cooker with water, put the oiled stones in, turn it on low, and let them heat for at least an hour, or until heated through.

After a hot bath, lie on clean sheets and put the warmed oiled rocks on certain parts of your body such as your stomach, chest, forehead, legs, feet, and so on.

The warm pressure of the heated stones will soothe aching muscles while you enjoy this unique ritual.

Don't forget to learn from children. The simple lessons in life are right there for all to see.

When was the last time
you sang out loud?

Think about this: How many of your actions are controlled by love and how many are controlled by fear?

Smile at passersby as you
walk down the street.

$\mathcal{L}$ong walks on the beach aren't just for summer! Bundle up and take a walk along the shoreline on a winter's day.

$\mathcal{L}$ook up! You never know
what you might be missing.

Have an after-midnight shopping adventure! Take advantage of the twenty-four-hour superstores and go shopping at odd hours when hardly anybody is there—you can have the aisles to yourself and browse to your heart's content.

"*Every time I've done something that doesn't feel right it's ended up not being right.*"

—Mario Cuomo

Trust your gut instincts.

*L*ook inward—the answers you need to life's questions are inside you. The hard part comes when you have to act on that information.

Jump rope and embrace the kid in you. Don't forget to sing your favorite rhymes!

Whistle your favorite tune.

Learn to say
"I love you"
in French.

$\int$ pend a few hours
paging through trashy
gossip magazines—the kind
you normally wouldn't get
caught dead reading!

*"God made the world round
so we would never be able to
see too far down the road."*

—Isak Dinesin

Always look for the silver
lining—a positive attitude is
worth its weight in gold.

Babe Ruth struck out
1,330 times.

*"Character consists of what
you do on the third and
fourth tries."*

—James A. Michener

There is no shame in failure. The only shame is in not trying at all.

Kitchen Shortcut

Quick Pasta with Cauliflower

¼ cup good-quality olive oil
2 cloves garlic, peeled and minced
1 28-ounce can of peeled plum
    Italian crushed tomatoes
¼ cup raisins
¼ cup pignoli nuts
Salt and pepper to taste
1 head of cauliflower broken into
    small florets, steamed
1 pound cooked ziti or rigatoni

1. Heat olive oil in a large sauté pan. Add garlic, crushed tomatoes, raisins, pignoli nuts, and salt and pepper and simmer for 10 minutes. Stir in the steamed cauliflower and simmer for 10 more minutes.
2. Pour sauce over the cooked pasta and toss to blend. Serve in bowls with fresh grated cheese and crusty garlic bread.

One of our most neglected or underappreciated senses is our sense of smell. Scents from our everyday lives can spark memories and warm feelings.

Think about your favorite smells and recreate one in your home today: bread baking, chamomile tea, a squirt of fresh lemon, cutting into a fresh juicy orange, your dad's aftershave, your grandmother's peppermint Lifesavers, fresh ground coffee, fresh-cut Christmas trees, cinnamon sticks, vanilla beans . . .

Make a tape of all the songs that were popular when you were younger. Play it and sing along.

Send a funny card to someone
with whom you have lost touch.

Find a favorite quote and post it around your house, in the office, or in your car.

Get down and dirty:
Herb gardens aren't just for
backyards! Why not create
one for your windowsill? The
fragrant herbs will lend fresh
scents to your kitchen and
extra flavor to your meals.

*G*ive your green thumb a try
and plant a vegetable garden—
tomatoes, zucchini, corn.
Share the bounty with
family and friends.

"I have lived to thank God
that all my prayers have not
been answered."

—Jean Ingelow

Escape Monday madness: After a long day, unplug the phone, and take a few hours of quiet time.

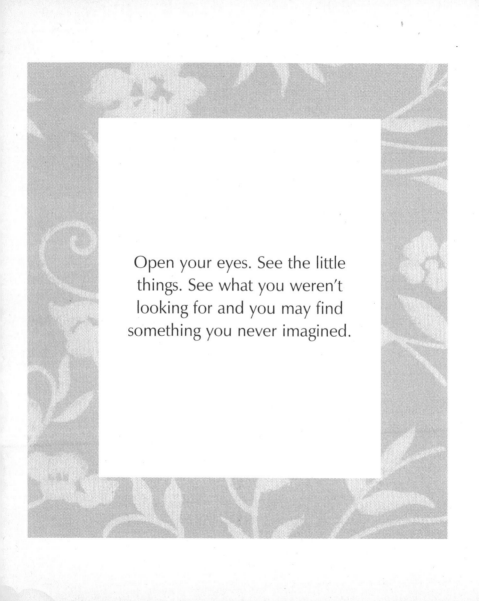

Open your eyes. See the little
things. See what you weren't
looking for and you may find
something you never imagined.